TG118122

THE LITTLE BOOK ABOUT

BREAD

Published in 2022 by OH!
An Imprint of Welbeck Non-Fiction Limited,
part of Welbeck Publishing Group.

Based in London and Sydney.
www.welbeckpublishing.com

Disclaimer:
This book is intended for general informational purposes only and should not be relied upon as recommending or promoting any specific practice, diet or method of treatment. It is not intended to diagnose, advise, treat or prevent any illness or condition and is not a substitute for advice from a professional practitioner of the subject matter contained in this book. You should not use the information in this book as a substitute for medication, nutritional, diet, spiritual or other treatment that is prescribed by your practitioner. The publisher makes no representations or warranties with respect to the accuracy, completeness or currency of the contents of this work, and specifically disclaim, without limitation, any implied warranties of merchantability or fitness for a particular purpose and any injury, illness, damage, death, liability or loss incurred, directly or indirectly from the use or application of any of the contents of this book. Furthermore, the publisher is not affiliated with and does not sponsor or endorse any uses of or beliefs about in any way referred in this book.

ISBN 978-1-80069-011-0

Compiled and by: Susan Clark
Editorial: Victoria Denne
Project manager: Russell Porter
Design: Tony Seddon
Production: Jess Brisley

A CIP catalogue record for this book is available from the British Library

Printed in China

10 9 8 7 6 5 4 3 2 1

Illustrations: Freepik.com

THE LITTLE BOOK ABOUT
BREAD

BAKED TO PERFECTION

CONTENTS

INTRODUCTION

If you're not thinking about it, you're eating it, and if you're not eating it (yet), that's only because it needs another five minutes in a very hot oven.

If you've got bread on your mind in between all the times you've just tucked into a slice, then this *The Little Book About Bread* is written especially for you. It not only celebrates all the wonders of bread in all its marvellous forms, but takes you to a new and very special place that only people who love bread can enter: Breadtopia.

However, while Utopia is an imagined perfect place, Breadtopia is an actual perfect place where all you have to think about is bread: when to eat it, how to make it, where to buy it, when to share it and when to keep it to yourself.

Without bread, there would be no civilisation as we know it - you can't exactly drag your nomadic tent around with pockets full of gloopy gruel! And without bread we would not have a multitude of "odes to bread" to linger over as we raise a slice of hot buttered toast to our lips before we start a busy day. *The Little Book About Bread* shares lots of these throughout its pages.

We may be little, but we've crammed an encyclopaedia's worth of bread facts, trivia and love into these wee pages; from a romp through the magical history of bread to a meander through the art, novels, songs and poetry that reflect our love of bread back to us.

The Little Book About Bread is practical too! It's full of hints and insider tips for those wanting to bake their own breads, and while not a recipe book as such, we've sneaked some recipes in so you can get started if you're a beginner.

Little, yes, but large when it comes to shouting about the joy of bread in all its many global guises. This is the book for all of us who love bread and don't care who knows it …

CHAPTER
ONE

Alchemy

The story of bread

"

Without bread all is misery.

"

William Cobbett, 18th-century
British farmer, pamphleteer and MP

66

Bread is for us a kind of successor to the motherly breast, and it has been over the centuries responsible for billions of sighs of satisfaction.

99

Margaret Visser

"

Here is bread, which strengthens man's heart, and therefore is called the staff of Life.

"

Matthew Henry

No Fire, No Bread

Somewhere between 400,000 and a million years ago, human beings first learned to control fire.

It could have been earlier or a little bit later – the evidence is scant so we can never know for sure. But what we do know, categorically, is this: no fire, no bread.

ALCHEMY

No Grains, No Bread

There's evidence of humans
gathering wild grains at least
100,000 years ago but no sign
of these grains being ground
until around 30,000 years ago.

We know this happened
because scientists have found
starch residues on stones dating
back to that time.

14

No Cooking, No Bread

We have archaeological proof of humans cooking bread that dates back to 14,000 years ago thanks to the discovery at a site in Jordan of two large stone fireplaces that both contained the charred remains of breadcrumbs.

Along Came Farming

We have evidence that some of the earliest bread crops were being grown in the ancient Levant region – an area that includes the Middle East and the Eastern Mediterranean – as long ago as 9,500 BCE

Those crops included wheat, barley, rye, lentils, chickpeas and flax – all crops which produce grains that you can use to make breads.

At this time, there is also growing evidence of dedicated ovens being built and used.

The Earliest Bread

The first breads are thought to have been made in or around 8000 BCE in the Middle East, and more specifically Egypt.

Grain was crushed using a quern – the first known grinding tool - and our ancestor bakers produced what we would now recognize, roughly, as chapatis (India) or tortillas (Mexico).

The first breads were unleavened; meaning no yeast or alternative raising agent was used.

The First Doughs

Flatbreads are made with flour, water and salt. This mix is then rolled into a flattened dough.

Although many flatbreads are unleavened, some, such as pizza and pita breads, do include a raising agent.

Flatbreads can be baked in the oven, fried in hot oil, grilled over hot coals, cooked on a hot griddle and eaten fresh or frozen to eat later.

10 Fascinating Flatbreads

Arepa - from Colombia and Venezuela

Bannock - Celtic unleavened bread from the British Isles

Bataw - Egyptian, made from barley, corn or wheat

Kitcha - as used in the traditional chechebsa dish from Ethiopia

Lavash - Armenian flatbread included on the UNESCO Intangible Cultural Heritage lists

Matzo - Jewish

Rieska - traditionally made from barley in northern Finland

Roti - South Asian, including Chapati and Dalpuri

Tortilla - a Mesoamerican/Mexican flatbread

Tortilla de rescoldo - Chilean unleavened bread, baked in the coals of a campfire

> **"**
> Better is bread with
> a happy heart
> Than wealth with
> vexation.
> **"**

Amenemope, Egyptian pharaoh of the 21st Dynasty

"

Bread's role as a staple food has paradoxically made it both sacred and banal, holding a place in our myths, folklore, and fairy tales as securely as it holds a place on our tables. It is holy, and yet humble.

"

Rose Williamson

"

It isn't bread that feeds you; it is life and the spirit that feed you through bread.

"

Angelus Silesius

Flatbread Recipe

A naan-style flatbread that you can eat plain or filled.

Ingredients

Makes six large flatbreads

450g/1lb strong bread flour, plus a little extra for rolling and dusting

1 teaspoon of baking powder

½ teaspoon of salt

2 teaspoons of dried active yeast (7½oz/ ¼ sachet)

2 teaspoons caster sugar

150ml (5 fl oz) tepid milk

30ml (1 fl oz) vegetable oil

150g (5oz) natural yoghurt, lightly beaten

1 egg, beaten

Clarified butter for brushing

continued overleaf

Method

Mix the flour and baking powder in your mixer bowl. Add the salt to one side and the yeast to the other (salt can kill the yeast, so try to keep them separated).

Dissolve the sugar in the tepid milk and add to the bowl, along with the oil, yoghurt and egg. Mix to make a dough ball.

Knead the dough by hand or use a dough hook set to slow speed for 10 minutes if you have a mixer.

Make sure you stop the mixer to scrape the dough stuck to the sides and bottom of the mixing bowl back into the main dough ball.

Once your dough looks smooth and satiny, shape it into a ball with lightly oiled hands and transfer to the proving bowl.

Cover with a clean tea towel and set to one side out of draughts to rise. Wait for it to double in size.

Stuff and Fry

Knock the dough back to release the trapped air and knead by hand for a second time but only for a few minutes.

Divide into 6 or 8 equal-sized balls.

You can now fry the breads if they are to make plain flatbreads or get creative and start stuffing them before frying.

Before frying, roll out your plain (or stuffed) dough balls, one at a time, on a floured work surface. Aim for a 23cm (9in) round for smaller flatbreads and 30cm (12in) round for larger ones.

Heat a large, heavy-based pan over a very high heat and dry fry your breads, one at a time, until large bubbles appear on the surface. This should take no more than 2 minutes.

Flip over and repeat on the other side until golden brown.

Brush with clarified butter while warm and serve with your main course.

Season & Stuff

You can easily season or stuff your flatbreads.
Make this fennel-chilli mix to scatter over the
dough halfway through the rolling process and
then fry the flatbread as normal.

Ingredients

1 tablespoon fennel seeds
1½ teaspoons chilli flakes
½ teaspoon sea salt

Method

Dry-fry the fennel seeds until they pop and
then transfer to a mortar or another sturdy dish
where you can crush them with the chilli and
sea salt.

Aim for a medium-coarse spice mix.

Etymology

It's thought the word "bread" relates to the word "brew", or it may come from the word 'break', meaning "broken piece" or "morsel".

"Bread" did not come into common use in the English language until 1200 CE, when it replaced the old word for bread which was: *hlaf.*

Old Danish – *brød*

Old German – *brot*

Old Dutch – *brood*

Old Norse – *brauø*

The slang use for "bread" or "dough" to mean money started in the 1940s.

The First Bread Recipe

It was not until Tudor times that the first printed bread recipe made its debut with the publication of a cookery book called *The Good Huswife's Handmaide for the Kitchen* in 1594.

By this time, bread was often made in large slabs that were allowed to go stale so they could be used as a serving dish.

This was called a Trencher but could only be used to serve foods that did not contain liquid.

Let the Devil Out

In the 19th century, it was believed that a cross slashed atop your bread let the devil out while it baked in the oven.

It was also believed that the symbolism can be interpreted as blessing the bread and giving thanks.

Along Came Yeast

Another massive leap forward in breadmaking was the discovery that the addition of live yeast to the bread produced carbon dioxide gas, which made the bread rise.

The ancient Egyptians were the first civilisation to harness what must have seemed like the magical powers of yeast, and by 1350 BCE had become the first peoples to brew beer and make yeast breads.

Which came first... the beer or the bread?

Nobody knows for sure, but either the first yeast breads were a by-product of brewing with some of the beer foam being skimmed into bread doughs, or vice versa, with the residual fermentation from making bread being skimmed off and combined with water to make beer.

More Bread Milestones

Foccacia – Made by the Etruscans (Northern Italy) in the 6th to 5th centuries BCE

Pretzels - Invented by European monks in the 6th century BCE

Bagels - Created in Poland by Ashkenazi Jews in the 1400s

Baguettes - First developed in 18th-century Paris, later refined and first named "baguette" in 1920

CHAPTER
TWO

Knead to Know

How to make great bread

"

There is nothing that is
not beautiful about bread.
The way it grows, from
tiny grains, from bowls on
the counter, from yeast
blooming in a measuring
cup like swampy islands.

Eleanor Brown, author of *The Weird Sisters*

66

There is no chiropractic treatment, no Yoga exercise, no hour of meditation in a music-throbbing chapel, that will leave you emptier of bad thoughts than this homely ceremony of making bread.

99

M.F.K. Fisher, *How to Cook a Wolf*

Basic Bread Recipe

This recipe will make two large or three smaller loaves. Once you have mastered it you can use it as the basis for numerous variations and even start creating your own unique Master Baker breads.

Ingredients

1kg/2.2lbs flour

10g (⅓oz) powdered dried yeast

20g (¾oz) fine salt

700ml (25 fl oz) warm water

Tablespoon of semolina for coating your loaves

You may like to bake a sprinkle of seeds or other enhancements into your artisan loaves

Method

You want to make a nice sticky dough that will be easy to knead. Expect messy hands and invest in a dough scraper.

This "one-stage" method is perfect to get you started making your own delicious breads.

Make your bread dough by combining the flour, yeast and salt in a large mixing bowl.

Start to add the warm water to activate the dried yeast and begin mixing the ingredients by hand to make a rough dough.

How To Knead

Sprinkle a light dusting of flour onto the clean work surface where you plan to knead.

Turn your sticky bread dough out of the mixing bowl.

Clean your hands.

Roll up your sleeves.

Ready, steady, go...

The Perfect Dough

You are aiming for a smooth and satiny dough, which will take you about 15 minutes.

You can throw your dough around in all directions while stretching it across your floured surface.

You need to break down the gluten fibres in the mixture and get air into the dough, which will help it rise.

Kneading is therapeutic, fun and a great stress-buster.

And here's the biggest secret of great breadmaking that most people never learn...

The Art of Folding

If there's one sure-fire way to get bigger air bubbles and lots more tasty character into your homemade breads, it is the closely-guarded secret of folding the dough.

And not just at the end of the kneading process.

Try folding the dough every 30 minutes as the dough is proving (rising) and see for yourself what a difference this will make to the quality of the finished bread.

How To Fold a Dough

Before your kneaded dough goes back into the bowl, fold it in half FOUR times.

Take hold of a chunk of the dough that is resting on the floured surface and fold it into the centre of the ball. Take just enough that you can easily fold the whole of the base back into the top of the ball in four different folds.

Turn the dough after each fold to grab a new section and when you have folded four times, your dough is ready for proving.

"

Bread takes the effort of kneading but also requires sitting quietly while the dough rises with a power all of its own.

"

David Richo, author of *The Five Things We Cannot Change and the Happiness We Find By Embracing Them*

Sitting Quietly

Once you have kneaded and folded your dough, put the dough ball back into your mixing bowl and cover the bowl with a clean tea towel or cling film.

Your dough will rise by itself if you leave it at room temperature.

You want your dough to double in size, which can take as little as 40 minutes or as long as four hours, so the lesson here is, breadmaking cannot be rushed.

It can, however, be slowed down by putting the covered bowl into the fridge, where you can leave it for a maximum of 48 hours.

Baking Insider Tip No.1

As you become more experienced and confident, you may want to prove your bread in a specially designed container called a banneton, especially if you are making sourdough. This will give you dome-shaped loaves like you see in shops and artisan bakeries where the top of the bread is covered in ever-decreasing concentric circles. These indentations are made during proving.

Baking Insider Tip No.2

For a professional-style bake, remove any oven shelves you are not using and place a deep roasting tray full of water in the bottom of the oven to create steam during the baking process.

Baking Your Bread

You need a really hot oven, so switch yours on to 230°C/440°F/Gas Mark 10.

Put your baking tray into the oven to get it super-hot.

Roughly divide your dough depending on how many loaves you plan to make. Cover these "chunks" of dough and leave them to rest for 15 minutes.

You will now be ready to shape your final loaves into the loaf tins or into balls if making bread rolls.

Grease and flour the tins you are using and if making rolls, make sure they are sitting on floured boards so you can easily get them off when it's time to bake.

This is also the time to coat your loaves or rolls with your chosen coating.

Semolina works wells because it gives a crunch to the baked crust.

Cover these with a plastic bag to retain moisture in the dough and leave to double in size again.

Wash Your Loaf!

A coating (wash or glaze) of something can make your bread look - and taste - extra special. Add with a pastry brush before you bake.

Egg - beaten whole egg, just yolk or just white all give different tones.

Milk - this will help colour the crust. Whole milk is preferable.

Water - as mentioned opposite, a spray of water makes the crust extra crisp.

Butter - this will soften the crust but give a richer flavour.

Honey/syrup etc. - another way to get a sweeter crust.

Into the Oven

Once your loaves have doubled again inside their loaf tins, moulds or on the baking tray, they are ready to go into the oven.

Transfer them to the baking stone or hot baking tray; slash the loaf tops with a serrated knife if you want to and then spray the top of each loaf with water to help keep it moist when it hits that hot oven.

Bake until the loaves look well browned and crusty.

When your loaf is ready it will sound hollow when you turn it out of the loaf tin and tap the bottom.

At-a-Glance Baking Timings

Rolls - 10-20 minutes
Small loaves - 30-40 minutes
Large loaves - 40-50 minutes

If in doubt, leave your loaves to bake to perfection a little longer.

Once your bread is out of the oven it needs to be cooled on a wire rack.

Insider Tip: You can serve your bread still warm, but if you want to slice your loaf it needs to cool completely.

"

I would say to housewives, be not daunted by one failure, nor by twenty. Resolve that you will have good bread, and never cease striving after this result till you have effected it. If persons without brains can accomplish this, why cannot you?

"

Housekeeping In Old Virginia,
Marion Cabell Tyree editor. (1878)

Bread as Therapy

There are so many ways that baking bread is good for the body, mind and soul. You will calm down, you will slow down (you cannot rush breadmaking) and most of all you will connect back to those parts of yourself you like the best but may have forgotten as you race through life.

There is nothing more therapeutic and sometimes more challenging than making bread, but you will only discover this truth if you try it yourself.

You will learn about you. You will learn about life. And you will learn to make GREAT bread.

LESSON ONE:
Accept failure

You will get lumpy bread, bread that does not rise, bread that tastes like bird seed. Bread that won't leave the tin.

You will not be happy. You will want to throw the tin and your inedible bread at the wall.

Don't.

There's something to be learned with every failure, and each time you learn a new lesson, you become a better baker.

Much like life, you need to roll (geddit?) with the punches and learn from disappointment.

You, like a nicely rising dough, can only grow from the experience.

LESSON TWO:
Give the gift of your time

Breadmaking cannot be rushed. Nature, not you, will be in charge of the various stages of the process, so if you don't really have the time to devote to it, then postpone your breadmaking until you can relax, give your all and enjoy the experience.

This is a GREAT lesson.

Bread is not impressed by your ability to do half a dozen tasks very badly, so stop.

They say when the student is ready, the teacher shows up.

If you're weighing out the flour and watching the yeast wake up then you should be able to work out who's the teacher and who's the student.

Zen, or what?

LESSON THREE: Give your love and kindness

And I don't mean just to the bread mix!

Making bread can teach us so many things if we stay humble enough to learn.

And one of the biggest lessons of all is that it is your attitude to the task in hand that will determine the outcome, whether that's breadmaking or something else you're giving your time and attention to.

Be the Change. Make the Change.
Live the Change.

Bake the Bread.

And do all of that with as much love as you can muster because once you've lived a lifetime you will be able to look back and see how much of that love came right back at you, in spades.

Bakers' Lingo

Banneton – traditional mould used to shape bread as it proves (rises). Makes pretty concentric rings in the dough ready for baking.

Bread stone – sometimes called a pizza stone, this is an oven-proof thin stone or ceramic slab which you pre-heat in a very hot oven.

Bran – the outer layer of wholegrains such as wheat or oats. Rich in both fibre and the B vitamins.

Crumb – the appearance of the inside of the bread; the size of the air holes and the pattern of their distribution.

Discard - this is what we call that portion of a bread starter that you remove to allow what's left to keep expanding.

Dough - mix of flour, water, salt and activated yeast.

Dough scraper - A flexible plastic tool that you use to scrape dough from the work surface back into the dough ball you are kneading and to shape that dough ready for proving. Do not attempt breadmaking without one!

Dutch oven - a large and lidded casserole dish (usually cast iron) which you can use to bake your loaf for the first half of its bake time.

Feeding the starter - you have to keep your sourdough starter alive by adding flour and water to the mix. (See S for Starter)

Fermentation – two processes that take place in the bowl when you make bread and before it goes into the oven. Yeast is activated when you add lukewarm water to the mix. The second process is the reaction of the flour to the water to develop gluten.

As a general rule, the longer the fermentations go on, the more depth and taste the finished bread will have.

Folding – a variation on kneading. Once you've stretched out the gluten fibres, if you fold the dough back into its centre in an orderly fashion, you realign the fibres, which, in turn, makes the dough less sticky and easier to work with.

Gluten – a general term for the proteins found in many grains but especially in rye,

wheat and barley. When you add water to flour you create gluten, which gives a dough its elasticity.

Kneading – a hands-on technique where the dough is pushed and stretched and pummelled and folded back in on itself to help develop the gluten. The more you knead, the more you will feel the dough become more elastic and smoother to the touch.

Knocking back – once your dough has risen and doubled in volume, you need to knock it back again to release some of the trapped air ready for a second proving.

Lame – basically a sharp razor blade in a protective holder which bakers use to score sourdough and make fancy patterns on the surface of the bread before it bakes.

Loaf tin – I would be worried if you need this term explained. Maybe use your loaf... as it does what it says on... the tin! Quite.

Oven spring – this refers to the expansion of a dough in the oven before the crust begins to form. It is the result of the yeast's final act of selflessness before it is finished off by the great heat.

Proving – this simply means allowing the kneaded dough to rise. Dough rises faster in warmer temperatures and as you become more experienced, you can experiment with slowing down and accelerating a rise by changing the surrounding temperature.

Signs of Over-Proving: Over-proved loaves will be flat. They have, effectively, over-inflated and then collapsed. Ooops!

Signs of Under-Proving: Under-proved loaves will be dense and still doughy in the middle.

Scoring – a series of shallow cuts into the top surface of your loaf to prevent it splitting or bursting when it is baking in the oven at high temperatures.

Shaping – you shape your bread before the second proving. So, if you are using a banneton, this is when the dough goes into the mould; if you are making bread rolls, you shape and place them on baking parchment. Use floured hands or your dough scraper to tuck the edges of the shaped loaves or rolls under themselves. This creates tension on the surface of the dough which then helps the loaf or rolls keep their shape.

Soda bread – traditional Irish bread that found a new fan-base during Coronavirus lockdowns because it does not need yeast to rise. With soda bread, the rise is created by using bicarbonate of soda and buttermilk, so there is no need to knead the dough either.

Sourdough – bread made only with flour, water and salt. The raising agent is wild yeast that occurs naturally; in the flour, in the surrounding atmosphere, and on the surfaces where the bread is worked. It has a slightly sour flavour, which is made more intense by a longer fermentation, and is more easily digested.

Sourdough starter – a live mix of fermented flour and water used to make sourdough breads.

Stoneground – flour that has been made from grain ground by stones is nutritionally superior to flours made by machines, which remove the wheatgerm and the bran grain husks.

Unleavened bread – any bread that is made without the use of a raising agent. Sometimes called flatbreads.

Yeast – a naturally-occurring microorganism that converts sugars to alcohol and carbon dioxide. This is the fermentation process that helps a bread dough rise.

Sourdough Starter Kit

Sourdough starter takes the place of yeast when you make your dough. It works because there is already wild yeast captured in the starter that has been feeding on the starches in the flour as you've nurtured and looked after the starter.

So, here's how you make and love your first starter.

Ingredients

An old aroma-free jam jar

60g (2oz) of good-quality flour; you choose the type. You can use a strong white bread flour or a hefty dark rye. You can even mix the two. Every new starter is different and every loaf you bake will be unique to you and the conditions of baking on the day.

60ml (2fl oz) warm water

Method

Mix the flour and the water in your jar, cover the top with cling film but make sure you pierce the film to make small air holes before leaving the jar to do its own thing somewhere where it will be warm and undisturbed.

After 24 hours, you should start to see bubbles, which tells you the culture is live and fermentation is taking place.

Now do... absolutely nothing!

Keep an eye on your starter and when you see a dark brown liquid starting to appear on the top of the culture, get ready to feed your new baby, but first drain this liquor off.

Smells Like Unwashed Feet!

This brown liquid is known as "hooch" and can smell like unwashed feet but it is a sign everything is doing what it should be doing.

If any of the culture itself is darkening with the hooch, scrape that out of the jar and discard it.

Hooch is a sign your starter is hungry, so now is the time to feed it.

Top your starter up with a tablespoon of your chosen flour and add a tablespoon of lukewarm water too.

Mix into the paste of the existing culture and leave to ferment.

Check your starter every day and feed whenever you see hooch appearing.

Volcanic Eruptions

If the mix threatens to spill up and over the jar at any point, divide it and start a second culture. Maybe be a little more experimental with this second starter and try combining different flours as part of the feeding.

After seven days, your starter is ready to help you make bread, so follow a favourite recipe.

If you've used up most of your starter, just feed the starter back up to its original levels.

Once you get the hang of this, you will probably need to keep your starter in the fridge to slow down fermentation and keep the hooch at bay.

Top Tools for Making Bread

Must Haves

Bowl/dough scraper

Bench knife

Silicone mat

Loaf pans

Thermometer

Weighing scales

Nice-to-have

Lame

Baker's baskets - bannetons

Dutch oven

Bread knife

Pastry board

CHAPTER
THREE

Good Breadmates

You won't want one without the other!

"

One of the more curious-among-most-curious things Alice found the other side of the Looking Glass was the ill-feted Bread-and-Butterfly...

"Crawling at your feet," said the Gnat (Alice drew her feet back in some alarm), "you may observe a Bread-and-Butterfly. Its wings are thin slices of Bread-and-butter, its body is a crust, and its head is a lump of sugar."

"

From Lewis Carroll, *Through the Looking-Glass and What Alice Found There*

Bread & Butter Soulmates

The perfect marriage of good bread with lashings of creamy butter has its own word in the German language.

Butterbrot means, literally, "buttered bread".

The act of buttering bread has its own word too: *Buttenadting*.

Star Gazing & Bread Buttering

Many believe it was the early 16th century astronomer Nicolaus Copernicus who first thought to butter bread.

Sadly, this cannot be true since the Oxford English Dictionary has a reference to buttered bread dating back to 1496.

66

I like bread, and
I like butter - but
I like bread with
butter best.

99

Sarah Weiner, author of *The Slow Food Companion*

66

She remembered a restaurant she'd gone to in San Francisco, years before. Delfina? That was it. She'd had delicious sourdough bread there, painted with butter.

99

Beth Harbison, *The Cookbook Club: A Novel of Food and Friendship*

66

Honest bread is very well – it's the butter that makes the temptation.

99

Douglas Jerrold (1803–1857)

Bread & Butter Pickles

Delicious with a slice of bread and butter,
bread and butter pickle is said to have
been the brainchild of cucumber farmers
Omar and Cora Fanning, who started
selling "Fannings Bread and Butter Pickles"
during the Great Depression of the 1920s.

It is said the name for this jar of
fermented cucumbers originated when the
couple bartered them for the food staples
they could no longer afford, including
bread and butter.

"

If thou tastest a crust of bread, thou tastest all the stars and all the heavens.

"

Robert Browning (1812-1889), English poet

Bread & Cheese

According to Queen Elizabeth I, the Virgin Queen who was the last of the five Tudor monarchs:

66

A meal of bread, cheese and beer constitutes the perfect food.

99

Actor, Daniel Radcliffe, aka
Harry Potter, has described
his diet as being that of a
19th-century Irish navvy, apart
from the litre of stout each day.

66

It's meat and potatoes and
bread and cheese; those are my
four food groups!

99

"

Bread is the staff of life.

"

Jonathan Swift

I'll Have Mine with Cheese

Humans have been combining bread and cheese for centuries. Even the Ancient Romans put together recipes for cheese melted on top of bread.

And all across America, you'll find creative takes on the grilled cheese sandwich which was formally created in the early 1900s.

66

I eat whatever
I want. I like bread
and cheese and
wine, and that
makes my life fun
and enjoyable.

99

Gwyneth Paltrow, American actress

The Sandwich

A dish of twin and sometimes even triple soulmates – two or even three slices of bread – glued together by an infinite variety of fillings.

But where did it start?

The clue lies in the name. The man who brought us the life-changing sandwich was John Montagu (1718–1792), who just happened to be the fourth Earl of Sandwich!

John "The Sandwich" Montagu

The original "fast food", the invention of the sandwich has long been attributed to a man who was such a profligate gambler he refused to leave the gaming tables for even a single second, and instead, asked his manservant to fetch him something that could be served between two slices of bread, thus enabling him to carry on gambling.

As a British statesman, he had travelled widely throughout the Eastern Mediterranean where he had much admired the practice of serving delicate finger foods between slices of bread or stuffed into grilled pita breads as part of a Greek or Turkish meze.

Before long the ladies of society had adopted the practice of serving dainty sandwiches as a supper food at their late-night balls. So, it would be more accurate to say what the Earl did was make the sandwich acceptable to High Society.

Imagine a Picnic Without a Sandwich!

It wasn't long before the idea of delicious bread with something even yummier wedged between two slices caught on in Georgian Britain.

By the 1760s, literary references to sandwiches began to appear and the sandwich became a fixture of suppers, picnics, lunches and as affordable fayre for weary travellers stopping at wayside taverns and inns.

66

I do like a little romance...
just a sniff, as I call it, of the
rocks and valleys. Of course,
bread and cheese is the real
thing. The rocks and valleys
are no good at all, if you
haven't got that.

99

Anthony Trollope, Victorian novelist

>> 66

It is only high up in the culinary scale that one finds delicacies spread on bread without the coffin lid which spells death to the flavour.

>> 99

H.D. Renner, *The Origin of Food Habits*, 1944

Mr Renner was clearly not a huge fan of the humble sandwich complaining, as he did, that when we eat, we feast first with the eyes and so, he went on to ask, how can a food with a hidden filling (a sandwich) excite the gastronomic palate?

Favourite Fillings
Britain's Top 5 Sandwiches

1. Bacon
2. Egg Mayonnaise
3. Sausage
4. Cheese and pickle
5. Tuna and mayonnaise

A survey of 2,000 British adults revealed a major shake-up in the annual sandwich popularity stakes in the two years between 2018 and 2020, with the cheese sandwich being toppled for the first time from first place.

Grilled Cheese Please!

The USA's Top 5 Sandwiches

1. Grilled Cheese (by a mile and across all generations!)
2. Grilled Chicken
3. Turkey
4. Roast Beef
5. BLT

In the USA where the New York Deli Sandwich has been raised to an art form, the fillings now ranked in the top five share nothing in common with those topping the sandwich charts in the UK.

M is for Muffuleta

Invented by the Italian immigrant families who moved to New Orleans, the Muffuletta deserves to be better known.

Made from a muffuletta loaf – a round Sicilian sesame bread which is similar in texture to the better known focaccia bread – this sandwich is piled high with green olive salad, Swiss cheese, ham, salami, provolone and mortadella.

> **"**
> Man cannot live
> by bread alone; he
> must have peanut
> butter.
> **"**

U.S. President James A. Garfield (attrib.)

66

I think there were not
in all the city, four
merrier people than
the hungry little girls
who gave away their
bread and milk on
Christmas morning.

99

Louisa May Alcott, *Little Women*

Sliced to Perfection

There is no question that mechanisation and the arrival of the bread slicer changed the world of bread forever.

With less mess and fewer crumbs to clear away from the breadboard, many households switched to pre-sliced bread, which makes it even more extraordinary that the inventor of the first-ever mechanised bread-slicing machine struggled to get his invention to the marketplace at all!

In 1917, Iowan-born jeweller, Otto Rohwedder started touting his bread-slicing machine around, but companies were not convinced housewives would make the switch.

Another whole decade was to pass before the Chillicothe bread company in Missouri installed the machine in one of its factories.

Within two years, 90 per cent of all store-bought bread in America was factory-sliced for convenience.

Toast: to cook, or brown food (especially bread) by exposure to a grill, fire or other source of radiant heat.

Is there any finer word in the English language?

The Best Thing Since Sliced Bread?

It's the world's fastest comfort food. But only if you happen to own a toaster and have slices to fit.

Just a few years after bread companies started installing mechanical bread-slicing machines, the Continental Baking Company in America introduced sliced Wonder Bread.

As more companies switched to pre-sliced loaves, sales of automatic pop-up toasters – first invented in 1926 by Charles Strite – went through the roof. By 1933, American bakeries were making and selling more sliced than unsliced loaves.

Chic But Very Elite

Most kitchens may have a
pop-up toaster today, but back
in the 1930s when they first
started to become popular they
were a luxury purchase.

Some toasters cost up to $25 –
the equivalent of almost $400
in today's prices.

66

Money is short and
it's clear that milk and
honey will not flow,
but there will still be
healthy bread and
decent jam.

99

Franz Muentefering, German politician

"

Just a glass of beer, a
piece of dry bread –
and in one moment the
brain is stronger, the
mind is clearer, and the
will is firm!

"

Fyodor Dostoyevsky, *Crime and Punishment*

66

Bread is the king of
the table and all else is
merely the court that
surrounds the king.
The countries are the
soup, the meat, the
vegetables, the salad
but bread is king.

99

Louis Bromfield, American novelist (1896-1956)

Lockdown Beer Bread

If a pandemic lockdown happens again you won't care because here is a genius three-ingredient recipe for easy, no-knead-necessary beer bread.

Preparation time: 10 minutes

Ingredients

Makes one small 1lb loaf

450g (1lb) self-raising flour

1 tbsp granulated sugar

330ml (11fl oz) Ruby red ale*

*You can switch the taste up or down depending which beer you use; a rich IPA will give a bitter sourdough taste to the bread; a golden ale will yield a more mellow flavour.

Method

Preheat the oven to 180°C/350°F/Gas Mark 4.
Line a small 1lb loaf tin with baking parchment.

Mix the flour and sugar in a large bowl. Pour in
the beer and mix to a batter.

The dough will be wet and fizz once the beer
is added.

Tip this fizzy mix into your prepared loaf tin
and bake for 50-55 minutes or until a golden
crust has formed.

Allow to cool a little before removing from the
tin and the parchment.

Tear and share with good cheese or a bowl of
hearty soup.

CHAPTER
FOUR

Breadheads

From poets to philosophers

66

With bread, all sorrows are less.

99

The fictional peasant character Sancho Panza from the 17th Century Spanish novel *Don Quixote*

66

Let there be bread...
Let there be justice for all.
Let there be peace for all.
Let there be work, bread,
water and salt for all. Let
each know that for each
the body, the mind and the
soul have been freed to
fulfil themselves.

99

Nelson Mandela

Bread & The Bard

Of all the famous writers, living and dead, who've celebrated our great love of bread across the ages, the most famous must be William Shakespeare, although you would never guess why bread played such an important role in his life.

When William was a small boy, his father was the bailiff of Stratford-upon-Avon where one of his most important jobs was to ensure the bread sold to the town's population was of good nutritional quality.

The Shakespeare Centre Library and Archive in the UK is still home to an ancient copy of the *Assise of Bread,* which dates from 1608 and which tells bakers and others what measures and weights they need to follow.

And it is clear from a passage in *Troilus and Cressida* that the Bard knew a great deal about making bread. We know this because the character Pandarus teases Troilus that the woman he is in love with, Cressida, will have to be approached with the same precise care needed to bake good bread!

"

How can a nation be great if its bread tastes like Kleenex?

"

Julia Child, American TV chef and author

Rock 'n' (Bread) Roll

If you remember the American band, Bread, who had multiple hits in the 1970s – including *Baby I'm-a Want You* and *Make It With You* – you may have wondered why a rock band would be called Bread?

The unforgettable name came to frontman David Gates when the band was stuck in heavy traffic. They were behind a truck with the words "Wonder Loaf"written on the side.

What's the best thing about a bread joke?

It never gets stale.

Bread of Heaven

In the Christian faith, Jesus told his followers: "I am the bread of life."

But what does he really mean?

You can survive for a long time on bread alone, and biblical scholars say when Jesus equated himself to bread, he was telling his disciples that believing in him is an essential part of gaining access to an eternal life.

"

Bread for myself
is a material
question. Bread for
my neighbour is a
spiritual one.

"

Nikolai Berdyaev, Russian philosopher

Breaking Bread

In the Muslim faith, the word bread is used to refer to food in general.

All food, including bread, is treated as a gift from God and one that the Qur'an states should be taken care of; nurtured, protected and used appropriately.

A timid girl suspicious of everything... except bread!

Jayne Eyre, the aggrieved and orphaned protagonist in Charlotte Brontë's dark and brooding novel of abandonment, misery and finally redemption, was suspicious of everyone and everything except, it would seem from this excerpt, a good old fashioned and honest slice of homemade brown bread.

66

A little before dark I passed a farm house, at the open door of which the farmer was sitting, eating his supper of bread and cheese. I stopped and said: 'Will you give me a piece of bread? for I am very hungry.' He cast on me a glance of surprise; but without answering, he cut a thick slice from his loaf, and gave it to me. I imagine he did not think I was a beggar, but only an eccentric sort of lady, who had taken a fancy to his brown loaf. As soon as I was out of sight of his house, I sat down and ate it.

99

Jane Eyre

"

There he got out the luncheon-basket and packed a simple meal, a yard of long French bread, a sausage out of which the garlic sang, some cheese which lay down and cried, and a long-necked straw-covered flask.

"

Kenneth Grahame, *The Wind in the Willows*

66

Take away my
bread and circuses
and all I'll have left
is my pitchfork.

99

Anonymous

"Bread and circuses" was a term coined by the Roman poet Juvenal around 100 CE to refer to the strategic diversions of the Roman rulers.

These included dispensing free bread and staging gladiatorial matches to distract the population in the hope it would stop them noticing and complaining.

66

Peace goes into the making of a poem as flour goes into the making of bread.

99

Diplomat and poet Pablo Neruda

Let them eat brioche...

'Let them eat cake' is the traditional translation of the phrase attributed to Marie Antoinette upon learning the peasants had no bread.

She is reported to have said "Qu'ils mangent de la brioche" shortly before she was guillotined in the French Revolution.

But while nobody has really ever found reliable evidence she said it, if she did, the true translation is not let them eat cake but let them eat brioche; a different kind of bread.

Brioche was considered as much a luxury at the time as cake and so it is just as callous as saying "let them eat cake".

The quotation was used – and has survived – as a sign of the spoiled Princess's frivolous disregard for the starving peasants of France and her lack of empathy with their plight.

Both allegations would evidently be true, but only if those words had ever issued from Marie Antoinette's mouth.

❝

My piece of bread
only belongs to me
when I know that
everyone else has a
share, and that no one
starves while I eat.

❞

Leo Tolstoy

66

The smell of good
bread baking, like the
sound of lightly flowing
water, is indescribable
in its evocation of
innocence and delight.

M.F.K. Fisher

Buttery Brioche

Brioches are light, buttery and utterly delicious. They are also easy to make at home, but you need to make sure your ingredients are very cold, so leave the dough to rest in the fridge overnight.

You can make large or small brioches and you can use a normal cake or loaf tin or large muffin cases.

Preparation time: 15 minutes

Allow 3–4 hours for the dough to rise

Allow 30–40 minutes, cooking time

Ingredients

Serves 6

15g (½oz) fresh yeast, or one sachet of dried yeast

2 tablespoons of milk, lukewarm

100g (3½oz) butter, softened, plus a little extra to grease the tin

250g (9oz) plain flour

4 eggs

1 teaspoon salt

50g (1¾oz) caster sugar

Method

Dissolve the yeast in the milk. Grease a 20cm (8 inch) brioche mould or deep cake or loaf tin with butter. Place the flour in a bowl and make a well in the centre. Pour in the yeast and milk mixture, 3 eggs, the salt and butter and sugar.

Mix by hand for 10 minutes or by machine set to a slow speed for 5 minutes.

The mix is ready when the dough is glossy and elastic.

Rest the dough overnight in the fridge and in the morning place it in the mould/tin, cover loosely with oiled cling film to prevent the dough sticking to the film and leave in a warm place to rise for three or four hours or until it has doubled in size. Preheat the oven to 200°C/400°F/Gas Mark 6.

Beat the remaining egg to make a glaze and brush it over the top of the brioche before it goes into the oven.

Bake for 30-40 minutes until golden brown and the tin/mould sounds hollow when you tap the bottom or, if using muffin cases, the base of the brioche itself sounds hollow when tapped.

Brioche du Pauvre

Also known as "Poor Man's Brioche", this recipe uses far less butter than the classic recipe and only one egg. Plus, there is no pricey yeast since the recipe relies instead on baking powder, which is cheaper.

Marie Antoinette, take note!

Preparation time: 10 minutes

Cooking time: 30-40 minutes

Serves 6

Ingredients

30g (1¼oz) butter, melted and cooled, plus a little extra put aside for greasing

1 egg, separated

30g (1¼oz) caster sugar

1 teaspoon salt

200g (7oz) plain flour

150ml (¼ pint) milk, plus a little extra to glaze

2 teaspoons of baking powder

Method

Preheat the oven to 180°C/350°F/Gas Mark 4 and grease an 18cm (7 inch) brioche mould or deep cake tin with butter. Whisk the egg yolk with the sugar and salt until light and frothy.

In a separate bowl, whisk the egg white until stiff and then fold this into the egg yolk and sugar mixture.

Stir continuously as you add the flour, butter, milk and baking powder, making sure you are mixing lightly but thoroughly.

Place the dough in your prepared tin.

Take the floured end of a wooden spoon handle and press this deep into the centre of the brioche dough to make a deep depression.

Brush a little milk gently over the dough to glaze and then bake for 30–40 minutes, until the brioche is golden brown and the tin sounds hollow when you tap the underneath.

Bread & Political Struggles

At the turn of the century, when women suffragettes in the West were fighting to get the vote, the phrase "Bread and Roses" was adopted as a political slogan and rallying cry.

It originated from a speech given by American women's suffrage activist Helen Todd.

Bread & Dignity

The notion of fairness (bread) and dignity (roses) as basic rights for all humans captured the imagination of poet James Oppenheim, who wrote a poem called "Bread and Roses" in December 1911.

By the following year, the slogan and the poem were picked up by striking textile workers in Lawrence, Massachusetts in their struggle for fair wages and better working conditions: a battle that became known as the "Bread and Roses strike".

And since then, the phrase has been used as a song title in 1976 by Judy Collins; in 1988 by John. Denver and in 1999 by Ani DiFranco and Utah Phillips.

Tuppence a Bag

The 1964 Disney film *Mary Poppins* featured a song that Walt Disney never could stop talking about.

"Feed The Birds" was sung by an old woman in London where she scratched a living selling bags of breadcrumbs to passers-by to feed the pigeons.

For years after, Walt would tell the Sherman brothers, who wrote the Mary Poppins' score, how that particular song had captured the simple beauty of an act of charity and told how his own life had started to be dictated by that mantra as he had begun to understand what the song was really all about.

Small Acts of Kindness

Walt believed the breadcrumbs for sale in the paper bags represented the small acts of kindness we can do for others when we take the time to stop and notice their needs, instead of being preoccupied by our own.

In the film, a bag of breadcrumbs for the birds costs just tuppence and in Walt's newly formed world view, he understood that tuppence was really nothing to spend or spare and that what the song was really saying was that whatever your own circumstances, you could carry out charitable acts in the service of others by investing even a small amount of your time, your love, your money or your talent.

A Bread Bed

In 1980, the well-known British artist Antony Gormley used 8,640 slices of "Mothers Pride" bread which he first dried out and then dipped in paraffin wax to make an art installation called "Bed" which explored the idea that as one thing (the bread) rots away, another gains life (the mould).

> **"**
> Bread is like
> dresses, hats and
> shoes – in other
> words, essential!
> **"**
>
> **Emily Post**

CHAPTER
FIVE

Breadtopia

The wonderful world of bread

Breadtopia

Topia - a place with very specific characteristics

Utopia - an imaginery place where everything is perfect

Breadtopia - a real place where bread rules!

"

Avoid those who
don't like bread
and children.

"

Swiss proverb

BREADTOPIA

the A *to* Z *of* **Bread**

A is for - Arepa

Arepa is a flat, round, cornmeal patty-style bread made from cornflour and eaten in Venezuela and Colombia. You can bake, fry or cook it on a charcoal grill. Popular fillings include grated cheese, ham, black beans, chicken salad and avocado, shredded beef or perico (Venezuelan-style scrambled eggs).

B is for - Bolo lêvedo

A speciality of the Azores archipelago off the coast of Portugal, these delicious breakfast treats resemble a giant English muffin but are bigger, sweeter and chewier. Portuguese communities living on the East Coast of the United States have made the bolo lêvedo popular in sandwich shops.

C is for – Carta di Musica

A Sardinian bread rolled so thin it is said bakers can read a sheet of music through the dough, hence the evocative name. Baked in sheets or large circles, carta di muscia puffs up and is sliced into two before being returned to the oven to become extra crisp. Usually eaten as a snack with wine and cheese.

D is for – Damper

This is a Australian bush bread that was traditionally cooked over the hot coals of a blazing campfire and it could not be easier to make. Mix flour, water, a little salt and milk to form a dough which you can pierce with a twig skewer for cooking over the fire.

E is for - Enset

Enset is not the bread but it is an extraordinarily ingenious part of the bread-making process in Ethoiopia where the finished "bread" is called kocho. Enset is a plant which is pulped, mixed with yeast and then buried for up to two years to ferment. Once ripe, this mix smells of cheese but tastes of flatbread.

F is for - Flatkaka

This one makes our list solely because of its memorable name! This is a soft, round, thin and dark flatbread made from rye and popular in Iceland.

G is for – Gata

Armenian Gata cakes – which are really sweetened breads – with their delicate decorations, Armenian script and diamond pattern shapes are a kind of glazed pastry. Styles vary between region, as do the fillings which can include nuts and dried fruits.

H is for – Hagelslag

This word roughly translates to 'hailstorm' and refers to the giant sprinklings that top a slice of bread that is so beloved of the Dutch they sprinkle them onto more than 750,000 pieces of bread a day, consuming more than 30 millions pounds of these sprinkles each year.

I is for – Injera

A sour, fermented flatbread enjoyed in
Ethiopia and Eritrea, injera bread has a
slightly spongy texture. It is traditionally
made from teff flour and is the national
dish in both these countries, where bread
on the table trumps any other foods that
may be present.

J is for – Johnnycake

Now a speciality from the Southern USA,
this bread is believed to have originated
with the indigenous Native American
people. It is made from a corn batter, the
consistency of gruel, which is fried on a
hot griddle or skillet.

K is for – Khachapuri

This Russian cheese bread is a popular Georgian breakfast dish where it is often served with eggs. A variation on the Italian calzone, an oblong-shaped individual portion of bread is filled with cheese and baked.

L is for – Lángos

This Hungarian/Austrian yeasted bread looks like a fat dough patty. Deep-fried, it is served warm with sour cream and cheese or ham, onion and parsley and is popular as a filling snack between meals.

M is for - Malooga

This flatbread is made from a yeasted dough which is kneaded, left to rise, cut into large rounds and then stretched out repeatedly. Warm ghee is spread over the dough with each fold and the finished round is stretched out one last time before baking in a tandoori-style oven.

N is for - Ngome

A basic flatbread from Mali made from millet, water and vegetable oil.

O is for - Obwarzanek krakowski

This yeast bread from Poland (and specifically Krakow) is made from strands of dough twisted together in a spiral to form a ring shape with a hole in the centre.

P is for – Poori

Poori is made from wholegrain dururm wheat flour, salt and water and deep-fried where it puffs up into a pillow shape, before gradually deflating. Pieces of poori are torn off and used to scoop up lentils, rice and other dishes.

Q is for – Qistibi

This roasted flatbread, which hails from Tartarstan, Urdmurtia and Bashkortostan, is made from a non-fermented dough and then filled – the most popular filling being mashed potato. After roasting, clarified butter is drizzled over the flatbread.

R is for - Röggelchen

A rye-based small pastry treat popular in Eastern Belgium and the Rhine, this is not the prettiest bread you'll ever feast your eyes on. It's made by baking two mirror-image pieces of dough together, so you could call it a twin treat!

S is for - Simit

Sometimes called the Turkish bagel and generally believed to be a forerunner of that style of bread, simit is an individual portion (like pita) of a circular bread garnished with sesame seeds and cut in half to allow for a filling.

T is for - Tsoureki

A delicious sweet bread that is popular in all the countries of the former Ottoman Empire. The Greeks call it Tsoureki but it goes by other names in Bulgaria, Romania and Turkey. Enriched with eggs and shaped into a circle from braided strands of the dough, this is a soft, moist and chewy bread that is usually made for annual festivals. It often includes spices such as cardamom.

U is for - Unicorn Bread

Always a hit with younger (and older) kids; unicorn bread has never been more popular. To convert a humble slice of white into a magical feast, simply toast, butter while hot and sprinkle generously with multi-coloured sprinkles.

V is for - Vánocka

A festive bread from Slovakia and the
Czech Republic, this is a leavened bread
that is traditionally baked for Christmas.
Enriched with eggs and butter, it is similar
to a French brioche but has nutmeg and
lemon rind added to enhance the flavour
and the colour.

W is for - Wagafi

This is a super-thin Iranian flatbread that
contains a higher proportion of flour than
normal breads.

X is for - YOU!

Nobody has yet named a bread, either
traditional or modern, that starts with an
"X", so why not get there first with your
own unique bread recipe!

Y is for – Yufka

This is a paper-thin, round-shaped unleavened flatbread from Turkey. Usually made from wheat flour, water and salt, it is used in sweet pastries with nuts and dried fruits or in savoury ones with cheese, meat and vegetables.

Z is for – Zopf

A Swiss/Austrian/German bread made from white flour, milk, eggs, butter and hyears and usually twisted or plaited. Folklore claims the shape arose because a Swiss widow would bury a plait of her hair when she buried her husband. Traditionally served for Sunday breakfast with butter and jam.

Bread consumption

The countries with the highest bread consumption were (in 2016):

USA: 14.7 million tonnes

China: 9.3 million tonnes

Russia: 8.7 million tonnes

UK: 6.2 million tonnes

Germany: 5.2 million tonnes

Egypt: 4.6 million tonnes

Italy: 3.9 million tonnes

Together, these seven nations account for approximately 41% of global consumption, with China emerging as the fastest-growing market.

CHAPTER
SIX

Celebrating Bread

From the humble to the holy

"

Good bread is the
most fundamentally
satisfying of all foods;
and good bread with
fresh butter, the
greatest of feasts.

"

James Beard, author of *James Beard's American Cookery*

66

Bread is a
celebration.

99

Lynne Rossetto Kasper

Simple pleasures...

Bread and butter is a combination so deeply loved and ingrained in our collective love of all things related to bread that one Californian wine maker has embraced the idea that a wine label which reads 'Bread and Butter' tells us just one thing: whatever is inside the bottle will be delicious!

This small producer, now offering a range of whites, reds and rosés under the 'Bread and Butter' label has one simple mantra: The best things in life are often the simple pleasures so why overthink or overcomplicate it?

Catwalk Banana Bread

American model Chrissy Teigen's banana bread is so delicious she was able to trade it during the 2020 Coronavirus pandemic lockdown after putting out a distress call on Twitter explaining she needed salad leaves.

She has written two cookbooks and shares her spectacular banana bread recipe in her book, *Cravings: Hungry for More*.

Her secret ingredients?

Chocolate chunks and coconut flakes.

Cheesy Party Bread
Ingredients

1 loaf of round sourdough or any other
round bread

225g (8oz) mozzarella cheese

4 tablespoons butter

1 teaspoon minced garlic

1 teaspoon Herbes de Provence

Method

Preheat the oven to 180°C/350°F/Gas mark 4. Using a serrated bread knife, cut the bread into diagonal slices, but take care to stop a good inch from the bottom so the loaf stays intact. Place the cut loaf on a baking sheet.

Cut the mozzarella cheese in small ½ inch pieces and slide these into the bread cuts, again making sure you keep the loaf intact.

In a small bowl, melt the butter and stir in the garlic and herbs. Drizzle this butter mixture over the whole loaf.

Wrap the cheesy loaf in foil and place on a baking tray. Bake for 10 minutes. Unwrap and bake for another 10–15 minutes or until the cheese is bubbling and the bread is golden brown.

Vintage Oyster Loaves

Take little round loaves, cut off the top, scrape out all the crumbs. Put the oysters into a stew pan with the crumbs that came out of the loaves, a little water, and a good lump of butter; stew them together ten or fifteen minutes, then put in a spoonful of good cream, fill your loaves, lay the bit of crust carefully back on again, set them in the oven to crisp. Three are enough for a side dish.

Mary Randolph, *The Virginia Housewife*, 1824

"

In the history of art
there are periods
when bread seems so
beautiful that it nearly
gets into museums.

"

Janet Flanner, *Paris Was Yesterday*, 1925-1939

66

My father would slather fish paste on his toasted 'Mothers Pride' as we watched Grandstand.

99

Nigel Slater, British food writer

Bread Triggers Nostalgia

Thinking back to the bread that defined our childhoods can catapult us right back across the decades to a time and a place where we thought our parents were demigods who could do no wrong and where a crispy toasted concoction – my dad's favourite was savoury minced meat and baked beans – tipped out of the jaffling iron on a Sunday teatime was the foodie highlight of the week.

I've decided to dress as a different bread every day next week.

Roll on Monday.

The Jaffle Craze

The Jaffle iron, designed to create a toasted sandwich with tightly sealed edges, was invented by an Australian doctor called Dr Ernest Smithers, who named and patented his design in 1949.

It was a "must-have" accessory in any self-respecting family household of the 1950s.

Jaffle Trivia

The Jaffle iron is clearly a descendant of medieval waffle irons which were used to produce flat, unleavened cakes that were cooked in the hearth between two metal plates hinged together and flipped to make sure both sides of the waffle cooked.

Indoor camping171...

The jaffle iron I grew up with had somehow survived on into the 1970s.

It was battered and rusted but still did a sterling job on a cold winter's evening when my dad would butter two scraggy slices of white bread, fit one each side of the circular Jaffle iron, fill one side with some delicious filling, seal the iron by bringing its two sides back together again, trim what was left of the square-shaped excess bread away and plunge the Jaffle iron into the open fire in the drawing room.

It was like camping indoors and the queue for a jaffle toastie snaked out of the Drawing Room as far as the eye could see.

A lethal weapon...

It never occurred to me until now that the Jaffle iron could also double up as a superb weapon. And I only realise this because I found a headline that appeared in the *Illawara Daily Mercury* in December 1953 which read: 'Wife hit husband with Jaffle iron; fine £3'

I shouldn't be, but I am crying with laughter... and wondering if the satisfaction of a thwack smack was worth the fine.

And whether there was actually a filled jaffle in the iron when the assault occurred?

Which to my mind would be a waste of a very good supper snack.

Bread of Happiness

Bread of Happiness is a 2012 Japanese film.

The plot:

Rie and Nao own a bakery-cum-restaurant named Mani which is situated on the shores of Lake Toya, Hokkaido. Nao is the baker who bakes the bakery's bread, while Rie is the chef who prepares the food in the restaurant.

The shop attracts a variety of customers, many of whom are having personal problems. What's strange is that whenever they walk out of the shop they only feel one emotion: Happiness.

Is there a special ingredient in Nao's artisan bread? You'll have to watch the film to find out.

Clever and Eco-Friendly

Gail's bakery, which currently trades from some 70 locations in England, hit the headlines when it made its first loaf of Waste Bread in 2018 in a bid to cut down on food waste.

The tasty sourdough loaf is made by turning day-old unsold loaves into breadcrumbs, before making them into a porridge-type mix. This is added to a fresh white sourdough dough, resulting in a fresh loaf, with the recycled bread making up a third of its ingredients.

Waste Not, Want Not

Gail's has promised to expand its product range made from food waste in a bid to further recycle surplus ingredients from its supply chain.

Gail's has been working on 25 new products as part of its eco-conscious baking line as it moves towards a zero-waste business. A hot cross bun bacon buttie is among the new ideas.

What do
you call 52 slices
of bread?

A deck of carbs.

Are You a Carb Detector aka Bread Lover?

In 2009, scientists added the savoury taste sensation umami to the established list of those different elements humans can easily identify by taste, namely sweet, salty, sour and bitter.

Now, it seems, a sixth taste sense could be joining the list; one which might explain our love of bread.

Researchers at Deakin University in Australia published a paper in the *Journal of Nutrition* which challenged the idea that we crave carbohydrates because we crave sugar and suggested, instead, that some of us can directly detect the taste of starch, and that's why we like bread.

Dreams Can Come True!

We had the cronut (croissant/donut hybrid) and the cromuffin (croissant/muffin mix), but it wasn't until the croloaf followed that the dreams of many bread lovers finally came true.

An ingenious hybrid loaf made using all-butter egg pastry but constructed like a regular rectangular loaf of bread, the shape means the loaf slices easily for toasting.

Anyone for Cricket(s)?

A British bakery broke new baking ground at the end of 2018 when it launched a bread made from the ground-up protein-packed bodies of hundreds of crickets.

Using cricket flour supplied by an insect food brand company called Eat Grub, each Crunchy Cricket loaf contains around 336 crickets which have been dried, ground, mixed with wheatflour and grains and then baked to make what its makers describe as "a tremendously tasty and crunchy loaf".

Yum!

Oldest Bread Ever

Archaeologists have discovered what appears to be the birth of sophisticated cooking – at a Stone Age site in the Middle East, dating back some 14,400 years.

The food debris includes gazelle, waterfowl and hare bones, wild mustard seeds, charred tubers and fragments of at least three different types of unleavened flatbread.

Best Bread Bible

Get saving your pennies because the five-volume *Modernist Bread: the Art and Science* does not come cheap.

First published in 2017, and with over 2,600 pages, it gives us a new understanding of one of the most important staples of the human diet: bread.

Co-authored by Francisco Migoya and Nathan Myhrvold, this tome promises to bring the complete story of bread to life across its five hardbacked books.

BREAD RECORDS

Priciest

The most expensive loaf of bread in the world comes from the Costa del Sol, is gold-plated, decorated with edible flowers and costs almost €1,400 ($1,500).

The bread is the brainchild of Master Baker, Juan Manuel Moreno, who presented two 400g (14oz) loaves at the Madrid Fusion expo. Each loaf contained one gram of edible gold and silver in powder and flake form, and 20g (¾oz) of edible flowers.

Largest

According to the *Guinness Book of Records*, the largest loaf of bread ever made weighed 1.571kg (3,463.46lb) and was made by Brazilian baker, Joaquim Conçalves in Curitiba, Paraná, Brazil on 13 November 2008 in celebration of Guinness World Records Day.

Longest

The longest line of breads consisted of 7,370 breads baked by Tizimín and Cámara de Comercio de Tizimín (both from Mexico) in Yucatán, Mexico, on 6 January 2020.

The record-breaking line of breads measured 3,009.65 m (9,874ft 2.15in).

The main ingredients used to prepare the breads were:

Flour (2,600kg / 2.8 tonnes)
Eggs (12,500)
Milk (625 litres / 137 gallons)

It took more than five hours to assemble the line and measure it.

The Ultimate Selfie Loaf

The world's largest (not real) loaf is a huge fibreglass and steel installation that sits outside the American Pan factory in Urbana, Ohio.

For years, the giant wrapped, and packaged replica of a sliced white loaf looked like something time had forgotten, but in 2016 it was cleaned and revamped and is now a tourist magnet for those wanting to take an impressive bread-loving selfie.

When does
bread rise?

*When you yeast
expect it...*

Religious Breads

In Judaism, ritually important bread was kept in a portable House of God (a sophisticated tent known as the Tabernacle) before the first great stone temple was built in Jerusalem.

And of course, a special sweet plaited bread called Challah is eaten for Shabbat every Friday evening throughout the Jewish world.

Commemorating the Dead

In Catholicism, unleavened communion bread is regarded as part of the body of Jesus – and in Lebanese Arab Christian tradition, a special bread called qurban is still used in ceremonies to commemorate the dead.

A Bread and Salt Blessing

In many cultures, bread plays a key role in weddings.

In Poland, for example, The Bread and Salt Blessing is a sweet tradition where both sets of parents meet the bride and groom before the reception can start. One set holds a loaf of bread, sprinkled with salt; the other parents have a goblet of wine.

The bread is given in hopes that the bride and groom will never go hungry or be in need. The salt conveys that time may be difficult, but they must learn to cope with the struggles in their life and marriage.

The wine, as with the bread, give hope that the couple never goes thirsty and their lives be filled with joy and happiness.

Who's the Boss?

In a traditional Russian wedding, bread is used to help show who wears the trousers and who will be the boss in the new marriage.

Either during the ceremony itself, or at the wedding reception, the bride and groom are given a loaf of karavay (a small, round loaf of bread).

A wedding guest will hold the loaf for them as each is invited to take a bite.

Whomever takes the bigger bite is then considered the head of this new family unit.

Vincent van Dough

Yes, it's an actual thing and one that really took off during the 2020 Coronavirus lockdowns.

Bread art involves taking any kind of vegetables, herbs, candied fruit or even real edible flowers and arranging them in a pretty pattern or scene on top of your bread, prior to cooking.

Once you take your work of art out the oven, you're left with a very pretty Instagram-ready loaf of bread that's also been enhanced with fantastic flavours.

For inspiration follow:

@Konel_Bread

@vineyardbaker

@elisabetaskarra

The Germans Have It...

Germany has more bakeries and the Germans eat more varieties of bread than most other countries in the world.

According to the bread register of the German Institute for Bread (yes, that's a thing!), there are now more than 3,200 officially recognized types of bread in the country.

And German bread culture was officially added by UNESCO to its Intangible Cultural Heritage list in 2015.

"

With a piece of
bread in your hand
you'll find paradise
under a pine tree.

"

Russian proverb